Fun and Simple State Crafts

Fun and Simple
Southeastern
State Crafts

West Virginia, Virginia, North Carolina, South Carolina, Georgia, and Florida

June Ponte

Enslow Elementary
an imprint of

Enslow Publishers, Inc.
40 Industrial Road
Box 398
Berkeley Heights, NJ 07922
USA

http://www.enslow.com

This book meets the National Council for the Social Studies standards.

Enslow Elementary, an imprint of Enslow Publishers, Inc.

Enslow Elementary® is a registered trademark of Enslow Publishers, Inc.

Library of Congress Cataloging-in-Publication Data

Ponte, June.
   Fun and simple Southeastern state crafts : West Virginia, Virginia, North Carolina, South Carolina, Georgia, and Florida / June Ponte.
      p. cm. — (Fun and simple state crafts)
   Summary: "Provides facts and craft ideas for each of the states that make up the Southeastern region of the United States"—Provided by publisher.
   Includes bibliographical references and index.
   ISBN-13: 978-0-7660-2935-4
   ISBN-10: 0-7660-2935-2
   1. Handicraft—Southern States—Juvenile literature. I. Title.
   TT23.5.P65 2008
   745.50975—dc22

                                                2007014032

Printed in the United States of America

10 9 8 7 6 5 4 3 2 1

To Our Readers:
We have done our best to make sure all Internet Addresses in this book were active and appropriate when we went to press. However, the author and the publisher have no control over and assume no liability for the material available on those Internet sites or on other Web sites they may link to. Any comments or suggestions can be sent by e-mail to comments@enslow.com or to the address on the back cover.

Every effort has been made to locate all copyright holders of material used in this book. If any errors or omissions have occurred, corrections will be made in future editions of this book.

♻ Enslow Publishers, Inc., is committed to printing our books on recycled paper. The paper in every book contains 10% to 30% post-consumer waste (PCW). The cover board on the outside of each book contains 100% PCW. Our goal is to do our part to help young people and the environment too!

Illustration Credits: Crafts prepared by June Ponte; Photography by Nicole diMella/Enslow Publishers, Inc.; © 1999 Artville, LLC., pp. 6–7; Corel Corporation, pp. 9 (bear), 15 (dog), 27 (deer); © 2007 Jupiterimages, all clipart; © 2001 Robesus, Inc., all state flags; Shutterstock, pp. 9 (apple), 33 (pecans).

Cover Illustration: Crafts prepared by June Ponte; Photography by Nicole diMella/Enslow Publishers, Inc.; © 1999 Artville, LLC., map; © Jupiterimages, state buttons.

CONTENTS

Welcome to the Southeastern States! 4

Map of the United States 6

WEST VIRGINIA 8
   Coal House 10
   Monarch Butterfly "Stained Glass" Chip Clip 12

VIRGINIA 14
   Scary Monster 16
   Poe's Raven 18

NORTH CAROLINA 20
   Raptor Wall Hanging 22
   Arrowhead Bracelet 24

SOUTH CAROLINA 26
   Basket Weaving 28
   My Pirate Flag 30

GEORGIA 32
   "I Have a Dream" Rainbow Magnet 34
   Statue of Liberty 36

FLORIDA 38
   Florida Panther Diorama 40
   Funny Fantasy Found Object Spacecraft 42

Patterns 44

Learn More (Books and Internet Addresses) 47

Index 48

WELCOME TO THE SOUTHEASTERN STATES!

West Virginia, Virginia, North Carolina, South Carolina, Georgia, and Florida are the states that make up the southeastern region. These states are called southeastern region because of their location within the United States.

The geography of the southeastern states varies from the beaches and sandy coastal islands of North and South Carolina to the Appalachian and Blue Ridge mountains. The Great Smoky Mountains National Park is located in western North Carolina. The Great Smoky Mountains got their name from the hazy, smoky-looking mist that surrounds them. South Carolina's northern beach is called the Grand Strand. It is made up of rivers, bays, and islands. Florida has one of the longest marine coastlines of all the states. Crocodiles, panthers, and manatees are among the endangered species that live in Everglades National Park in Florida. A group of islands off the coast of Florida are called the Florida Keys. These islands have a warm climate with cool ocean breezes.

In Georgia, the Chattahoochee National Forest covers about 750,500 acres of land. There are more than 450 miles of forest trails to explore. Shenandoah National Park is in the northern part of Virginia. There are many overlooks on Skyline Drive, a long highway through the park. From these overlooks the Blue Ridge, the Allegheny, and the Shenandoah mountains and Massanutten Mountain can be seen. There are coastal plains in Virginia along the Atlantic Ocean and Chesapeake Bay. The Allegheny Mountains, part of the Appalachian Mountain range, are a major part of West Virginia.

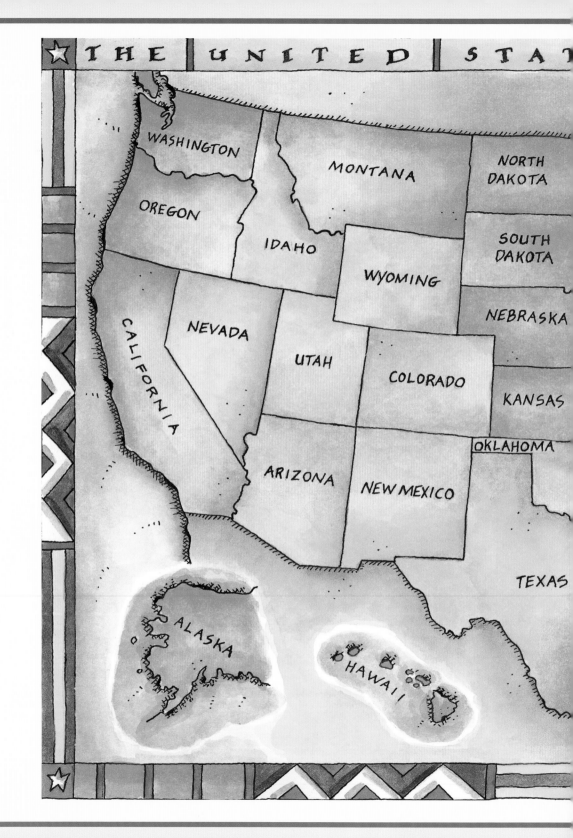

MINNESOTA

WISCONSIN

MICHIGAN

IOWA

ILLINOIS

INDIANA

OHIO

MISSOURI

KENTUCKY

ARKANSAS

TENNESSEE

MISSISSIPPI

ALABAMA

GEORGIA

LOUISIANA

FLORIDA

WEST VIRGINIA

VIRGINIA

NORTH CAROLINA

SOUTH CAROLINA

NEW HAMPSHIRE

VERMONT

MAINE

NEW YORK

MASSACHUSETTS

RHODE ISLAND

CONNECTICUT

NEW JERSEY

PENNSYLVANIA

DELAWARE

MARYLAND

WASHINGTON, D.C.

N

Southeastern States

WEST VIRGINIA

Origin of name	West Virginia was named for Elizabeth I, known as the Virgin Queen of England.
Flag	The West Virginia state flag is white with a dark blue border. In the center is a red ribbon that reads "State of West Virginia." Below the ribbon are two men who represent mining and farming. Between them is a rock that is dated June 20, 1863. This was the day that West Virginia became a state. Two rifles with a red hat that represents liberty are below them. The state motto, *Montani semper liberi*, which means "Mountaineers are always free," appears in a ribbon below them.
Capital	Charleston
Nickname	The Mountain State

Motto	*Montani semper liberi* (This is a Latin phrase that means "mountaineers are always free.")
Size (in area)	41st largest
Animal	black bear
Bird	cardinal
Fish	brook trout
Flower	big laurel
Tree	sugar maple
Industry	tourism, cattle, dairy products, corn, potatoes, poultry, apples, chemical products, coal and natural gas mining, primary metals, salt, stone, clay, and glass products

COAL HOUSE

In West Virginia, coal mining is an important industry. In Williamson, there is a house made completely of coal. The coal used to make the house was donated by local coal companies. The house was built in 1933 and weighs sixty-five tons. There are at least three buildings made of shiny black coal in the state, but the Williamson Coal House is the only house to be made entirely of coal. The building is now the home of the Tug Valley Chamber of Commerce.

What you will need

* shoe box with lid
* scissors
* black and green poster paint
* paintbrush
* markers
* blue and gold glitter pens
* brown construction paper
* ruler
* pencil
* white glue

What you will do

1. Turn the bottom of a shoe box upside down. Cut a door and windows in the side of the shoe box. Paint the shoe box black (See A). Let dry.

2. Paint the outside and rim of the shoe box lid green. Let dry. If you wish, draw flowers or grass on the front of the lid (See B).

A)

3. Using a blue glitter pen, draw the outlines of pieces of coal on the black painted shoe box. Let dry. Cut out a 1 1/2-inch x 4-inch rectangle out of brown construction paper. Print "West Virginia Coal House" on it in gold glitter pen. Let dry. Glue over the door to the house. Let dry.

B)

4. Place the house on top of the green lid (See C).

C)

MONARCH BUTTERFLY "STAINED GLASS" CHIP CLIP

The monarch butterfly is the state butterfly of West Virginia. These large butterflies are black and orange. The monarch butterfly drinks nectar from milkweed, dogbane, and goldenrod plants. Nectar is a sweet liquid that these plants produce. It serves as food for butterflies. Monarch butterflies born in the summer usually live for four to eight weeks. Those born in the late summer or early fall can live up to nine months. They have a wingspan of up to 4 ¾ inches! They are considered one of the most beautiful butterflies in North America. Make your own version of a Monarch. You can use any color you wish!

What you will need

* black construction paper
* pencil
* scissors
* red cellophane or plastic wrap
* white glue
* black pipe cleaner
* glitter pen
* clip-type wooden clothespin

What you will do:

1. Fold a piece of black construction paper in half. Draw half of a butterfly. (See page 45 for the pattern.) Cut it out (See A).

2. Trace the construction paper butterfly onto red cellophane and cut it out. Set the cellophane aside.

3. Fold the butterfly in half so that the wings match up. Cut out the inside areas.

4. Glue the red cellophane to the back of the butterfly. Cut a black pipe cleaner in half. Fold one half to make the antenna. Curl the ends. Glue the pipe cleaner the butterfly's head and let dry (See B).

5. Decorate the butterfly with a glitter pen. Let dry (See C). Fold the butterfly slightly, and glue to the clothespin (See D). Let dry.

A)

B)

D)

C)

West Virginia **13**

VIRGINIA

Origin of name	Virginia was named for Elizabeth I, known as the Virgin Queen of England.
Flag	The Virginia state flag is blue and has the seal of Virginia in the center. A man and a woman are shown in the center of the seal acting out the state motto *Sic semper tyrannis*, "Thus always to tyrants." A tyrant is a harsh, cruel ruler of a country. The woman with a sword represents Virginia. She stands over a fallen tyrant, whose crown lies on the ground.
Capital	Richmond
Nickname	The Old Dominion State

Motto	*Sic semper tyrannis* (This is a Latin phrase that means "Thus always to tyrants.")
Size (in area)	35th largest
Animal	American foxhound
Bird	cardinal
Fish	brook trout
Flower	American dogwood
Tree	flowering dogwood
Industry	dairy, poultry, tobacco, fruits, peanuts, coal, cattle, fishing, shipbuilding, chemicals

SCARY MONSTER

Professor Mark Cline is a Virginia artist who makes large monsters, dinosaurs, and many other kinds of statues. His Haunted Monster Museum is in Natural Bridge, Virginia, in a historic, old stone house. Cline created many weird and scary monsters. Make your own scary monster!

What you will need

* long or oval balloon
* flour
* water
* small bowl
* strips of newspaper
* 4 toilet tissue tubes
* masking tape
* poster paint
* paintbrush
* white glue
* glitter pens
* 2 medium wiggle eyes

What you will do:

A)

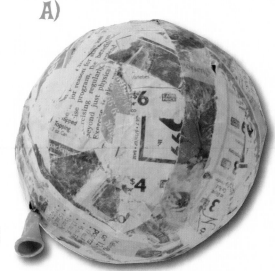

1. Blow up a long or oval balloon. Tie it off. Mix 1 cup of flour into 2 cups of water in a small bowl. Dip the strips of newspaper into the mix. Use your fingers to wipe off any excess. Cover the balloon with about four layers of newspaper strips (See A). Let dry overnight.

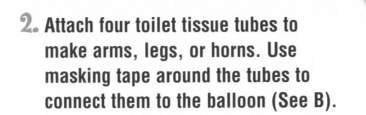

B)

2. Attach four toilet tissue tubes to make arms, legs, or horns. Use masking tape around the tubes to connect them to the balloon (See B).

3. Paint a monster face on the balloon. Let dry. Add touches of glitter over the paint, and let dry. Glue on two wiggle eyes. Let dry.

C)

POE'S RAVEN

Edgar Allan Poe wrote poems and horror stories. The Poe Museum in Richmond, Virginia, has many of Poe's letters, books, and other things that belonged to this famous writer. One of Poe's most famous poems is called "The Raven." The poem is about a large black raven that perches over the doorway to the poet's home. When the raven is asked questions, it only answers, "Nevermore!"

What you will need

* self-hardening clay
* 2 black pipe cleaners
* scissors
* 2 black craft feathers
* black poster paint
* paintbrush
* white glue
* wiggle eyes
* yellow construction paper
* glitter pen

What you will do:

1. Shape a piece of clay into a 4-inch-long egg shape. This is the body of the raven. Make another piece of clay into a 2-inch egg shape. This is the head (See A).

A)

B)

C)

2. Squeeze and flatten one end of the large egg shape to form a tail. Add two small triangle-shaped pieces of clay to the smaller egg shape to form an open beak. Attach the head to the body. Mold the egg shape to form the raven's body (See B).

3. Using a black pipe cleaner, make a foot with three toes by folding the pipe cleaner in half. Bend the doubled pipe cleaner three times to make the toes (See C). Repeat to make a second leg.

D)

4. Push the legs into the bottom of the raven's body. Carefully squeeze the clay tightly around the bird's legs. Let the clay dry overnight. Paint the bird black using poster paint. Let dry. Glue one feather to each side of the bird for wings. Glue on wiggle eyes (See D). Let dry.

E)

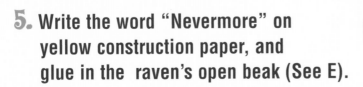

5. Write the word "Nevermore" on yellow construction paper, and glue in the raven's open beak (See E).

NORTH CAROLINA

Origin of name	North Carolina was named after King Charles I of England. The name Carolina is taken from the Latin word for Charles, Carolus.
Flag	The North Carolina state flag is blue, red, and white. The state initials, NC, in gold, with a white star that stands for North Carolina appear in the blue section of the flag. There are two dates shown above and below the NC initials. The top date, May 20, 1775, commemorates the day that the people of North Carolina met to declare their freedom from Great Britain. In North Carolina on April 12, 1776, the first official action by a colony calling for independence from Britain took place. This date appears below the state's initials on the flag.

Capital	Raleigh
Nickname	The Tarheel State
Motto	*Esse quam videri* (This is a Latin phrase that means "To be, rather than to seem.")
Size (in area)	28th largest
Animal	Eastern gray squirrel
Bird	cardinal
Fish	channel bass
Flower	American dogwood
Tree	pine
Industry	tobacco, cotton, sweet potatoes, soybeans, corn, peanuts, fruits, poultry, dairy, fishing, manufacturing, chemicals

RAPTOR WALL HANGING

Raptors are birds that hunt using their talons, or claws. Examples of raptors are owls, hawks, eagles, and falcons. The Carolina Raptor Center helps these birds and uses the birds to help teach environmental education. The center treats orphaned raptors, and raptors that have been hurt.

What you will need

* cream-colored poster board
* pencil
* hole punch
* brown yarn
* scissors
* white glue
* 2 large wiggle eyes
* yellow felt or construction paper

* 12-inch-long thin twig or dowel
* clear tape
* small craft feathers, natural white and brown

A)

What you will do:

1. Draw an owl shape on poster board. (See page 46 for the pattern.) Cut it out (See A).

2. Draw the owl's eyes and beak with the pencil. Punch a hole in the center top of the owl's head. Cut a 12-inch piece of brown yarn, and thread it through the hole. Tie a knot to make a loop for hanging (See B).

B)

3. Glue wiggle eyes on the owl's head. Cut a triangle-shaped beak out of yellow felt or construction paper. Glue the beak on the head (See C). Let dry.

4. Tape a twig horizontally to the back lower part of the owl. Starting at the bottom of the owl, glue on a row of feathers. Glue on the next row of feathers slightly above the first row, covering the ends of the first row of feathers. Repeat this step all the way to the head of the owl. Glue feathers around the eyes and beak (See D). Let dry. Ask an adult to help you hang the owl on the wall or in a window.

C)

D)

ARROWHEAD BRACELET

The Indian Museum of the Carolinas in Laurinburg, North Carolina, has thousands of early American Indian artifacts. An artifact is an object that people have made or used. These artifacts include pottery, jewelry, weapons, and tools. Some of the artifacts are over ten thousand years old! Make an arrowhead bracelet.

What you will need

* scrap paper
* pencil
* scissors
* self-hardening clay
* plastic knife
* elastic string
* poster paint
* paintbrush
* small, colorful wooden beads

A)

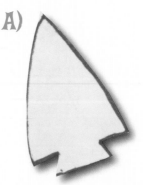

What you will do:

1. Draw an arrowhead shape on scrap paper. (See page 44 for the pattern.) Cut it out (See A).

2. Flatten a piece of clay until it is about 1/8 inch thick. Place the arrowhead pattern on the clay. Use a plastic knife to cut the clay

around the edge of the arrowhead shape. Make a total of six clay arrowheads (See B). Make a small hole with the point of a pencil through the top of each arrowhead. Let dry overnight. Paint the arrowheads bright colors. Let dry.

B)

3. Cut an 8-inch piece of elastic string.

4. String wooden beads onto the elastic string until you have enough to fit your wrist. Tie the ends of the elastic string together (See C).

C)

5. Cut six 5-inch pieces of elastic string. Thread a piece of elastic string through the hole in each arrowhead. Tie the arrowheads tightly onto the wood bead bracelet (See D). Cut off the extra pieces of elastic string.

D)

SOUTH CAROLINA

Origin of name	South Carolina was named after King Charles I of England. The name Carolina is taken from the Latin word for Charles, Carolus.
Flag	The South Carolina state flag is blue, with a white crescent and palmetto tree. The palmetto tree represents the fort made of palmetto logs that was defended by soldiers of South Carolina against an attack by the British on June 28, 1776. The crescent is the same shape as the emblem that the South Carolina soldiers wore on the front of their caps.
Capital	Columbia

Nickname	The Palmetto State
Motto	*Animis opibusque parati* (This is a Latin phrase which means "Prepared in mind and resources.")
Size (in area)	40th largest
Animal	white-tailed deer
Bird	Carolina wren
Fish	striped bass
Flower	yellow jessamine
Tree	palmetto
Industry	tobacco, soybeans, cotton, hogs, poultry, cattle, dairy, timber, paper manufacturing, chemicals, machinery

27

BASKET WEAVING

The Sea Islands are located along the coasts of South Carolina and Georgia. The Gullah people, who live on these islands, are descendants of people from the west coast of Africa. In the 1800s they were enslaved and brought to the area to pick rice. Today the Gullah community still has its own language and culture. The Gullah people are known for their traditions of storytelling, singing, and basket weaving.

What you will need

* square tissue box cut to about 3 ½ inches high
* scissors
* 26 yellow pipe cleaners
* 3 feet of ¼-inch wide light green ribbon

What you will do:

A)

1. Turn the cut tissue box upside down (See A). Place eight pipe cleaners across the bottom of the box. Hook the ends over the edge of the box.

2. Do the same thing in the opposite direction, weaving the pipe cleaners over and under. Weave five

rows of pipe cleaners around the sides of the box (See B). Twist two pipe cleaners together so they will be long enough to go around all four sides of the box.

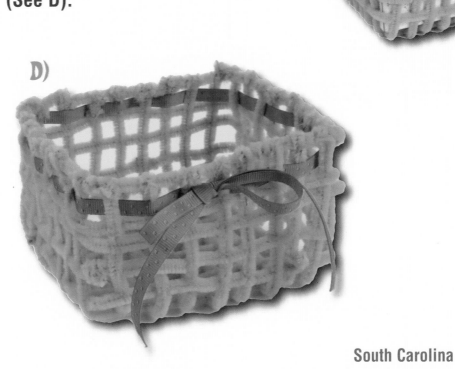

B)

3. Carefully remove the pipe cleaner basket from the box by unbending the pipe cleaner ends and gently pulling the basket (See C). Finish off the edge of the basket by twisting the ends of the pipe cleaners around the edge. Weave the ¼-inch light green ribbon near the edge of the basket, under and over the pipe cleaners (See D).

C)

D)

MY PIRATE FLAG

In the 1700s Blackbeard the Pirate attacked Charleston, taking ships and goods. Blackbeard was a tall man with a long black beard. Historians are not sure of his real name. It may have been Edward Teach or Thatch. Blackbeard liked to braid his beard. Legend tells us that he tied smoking cannon fuses to the ends of his braids to scare people. Blackbeard had a scary pirate flag with a skeleton on it and a heart.

What you will need

* pencil
* construction paper
* markers
* pipe cleaners
* white glue
* glitter pen

The skull and crossbones pirate flag is called the Jolly Roger. Create your own pirate flag and give it a name.

What you will do:

1. Think of a design for your pirate flag. Using a pencil, draw your design on the construction paper. Write the name of your pirate flag above the symbol.

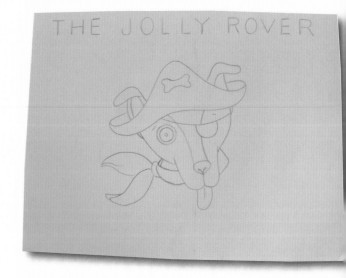

THE JOLLY ROVER

2. Use markers to go over the drawing, and color it in. Glue pipe cleaners to the edge of the flag. Go over the name of the flag with the glitter pen. Let dry.

3. Ask an adult to help you hang your pirate flag.

GEORGIA

Origin of name	Georgia was named for King George II of England
Flag	The Georgia state flag is red, white, gold, and blue. Thirteen white stars show that Georgia was one of the thirteen original colonies. Within the circle of stars are three gold columns holding up an arch that stands for the three branches of government. These branches are the legislative, judicial, and executive. A man with a sword is shown defending the Constitution.
Capital	Atlanta
Nickname	The Peach State

Motto	Wisdom, Justice, and Moderation
Size (in area)	24th largest
Bird	brown thrasher
Fish	largemouth bass
Flower	Cherokee rose
Gem	quartz
Tree	live oak
Industry	cotton, peanuts, pecans, peaches, manufacturing, textiles, paper, pulp, lumber, aircraft

"I Have a Dream" Rainbow Magnet

Dr. Martin Luther King, Jr., was born in Atlanta, Georgia, in 1929. King worked hard to help African-American people achieve equal rights in the United States. He wanted to make the world a better place. King gave a speech in which he spoke of his dream of a day when black children and white children would be friends. The rainbow is a symbol of hope and unity. Make a rainbow magnet. Write a word on each color of the rainbow to show what you think would make the world a better place for everyone.

What you will need

* light-colored poster board
* pencil
* scissors
* markers
* clear packing tape
* permanent marker
* white glue
* magnet

What you will do:

1. Draw a rainbow shape on light-colored poster board (See page 44 for the pattern.) Cut it out (See A).

2. Using a pencil, draw the stripes of the rainbow. Color the rainbow with markers (See B).

3. Cover the rainbow with clear packing tape. Trim any extra tape around the edges. Write a word on each stripe with a permanent marker (See C). Let dry.

4. Glue a magnet on the back (See D). Let dry.

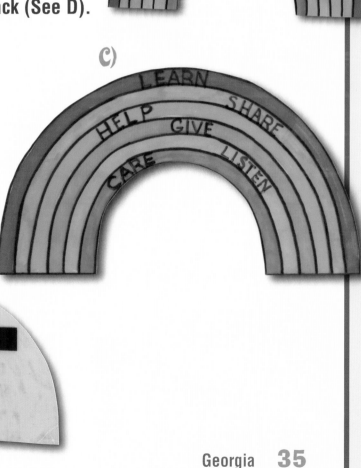

A)

B)

C)

D)

STATUE OF LIBERTY

In McRae, Georgia, there is a small Statue of Liberty. The original Statue of Liberty is located on Liberty Island in New York Harbor. It is 151 feet tall. The statue in Georgia is smaller, and stands thirty-five feet tall. The statue was made by Georgians, who used many different found materials to make the statue. It was made to remind people of the meaning of liberty. Make your own Statue of Liberty using things you have at home.

What you will need

* half-pint milk carton, washed and dried
* scissors
* light green construction paper
* white glue
* glitter pen
* aluminum foil
* toothpicks
* clear tape

What you will do:

1. Cut the top off of a clean half-pint milk carton. Place the carton on the light green construction paper. Trace the amount of paper you will need to cover the carton. Cut out the construction paper, and glue to the carton (See A). Trace the bottom of the carton onto

the construction paper, and cut out. Glue onto the bottom of the carton. Write "Statue of Liberty" on the side of the carton in glitter pen (See B). Let dry.

A)

2. Form the shape of the Statue of Liberty with her torch by pressing aluminum foil together. It should be about 6 inches tall. Cut three toothpicks in half. Put a piece of foil over the toothpicks. Twist the foil around the toothpicks into a point. Glue to the statue's head. Let dry.

B)

3. Tape or glue the statue to the green base (See C). Let dry.

C)

FLORIDA

Origin of name	The name Florida comes from the Spanish language and means "feast of flowers."
Flag	The Florida state flag is white with a large red X. In the center of the flag is the state seal. It represents Florida's culture and landscape with a Seminole Indian, flowers, a steamboat on the water, the sun, and a palmetto tree.
Capital	Tallahassee
Nickname	The Sunshine State

Motto	In God We Trust
Size (in area)	22nd largest
Bird	mockingbird
Animal	Florida panther
Fish	Florida largemouth bass
Flower	orange blossom
Tree	sabal palm
Industry	citrus fruit, vegetables, cattle, dairy, sugar cane, phosphate, tourism, printing, publishing, transportation equipment, machinery, electronics, plastics

FLORIDA PANTHER DIORAMA

The Florida panther is the state's official animal. It is considered an endangered species because there are less than one hundred panthers remaining in the wild. There are few wild places left for panthers to live. The Big Cypress National Preserve and the Fakahatchee Strand State Preserve in Florida have conserved more than 645,000 acres of land on which panthers can live.

What you will need

* self-hardening clay
* poster paint
* paintbrush
* white glue
* small wiggle eyes
* shoe box
* yellow construction paper
* pencil
* scissors
* dark green pipe cleaners
* light and dark green tissue paper

What you will do:

1. Roll a piece of clay into a 1-inch x 4-inch cylinder. Roll a ball of clay that is about 1 inches wide for the panther's head (See A). Add bits of clay to the head to form ears and

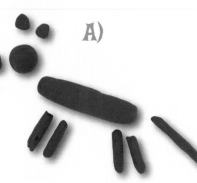
A)

B)

a nose. Attach to the body. For the tail, roll a 3-inch-long thin piece of clay. Attach it to the other end of the body. Make four legs that are about 1 ¼ inches tall. Add them to the panther's body (See B). Let the clay dry overnight.

C)

2. Paint the panther light brown. Let dry. Glue wiggle eyes to the head (See C). Let dry.

3. Paint the inside back of the shoe box blue and the bottom green. Let dry. Draw and cut out a yellow circle from the construction paper and glue it in the blue sky (See D). Let dry.

D)

4. Cut eight dark green pipe cleaners in half. Set aside eight halves. Cut the remaining eight halves in half again. Twist these small pieces of pipe cleaner onto the larger pieces to form plants with branches. Cut out leaf shapes or rip pieces of green tissue paper, and glue them to the pipe cleaner branches. Let dry. Twist the bottom of each pipe cleaner plant into a circle, and glue on the inside bottom of the shoe box. Let dry.

E)

5. Place the panther among the plants (See E).

FUNNY FANTASY FOUND OBJECT SPACECRAFT

NASA's Kennedy Manned Space Flight Center is in Cape Canaveral. Many spacecrafts have taken off from Cape Canaveral. These spacecrafts are different shapes. Imagine that you need a spaceship to fly to an interesting planet. Make one from things you find around the house. You can use crafts items, too, if you wish. Be sure to get permission from an adult for any materials you use.

What you will need

* 2 heavy paper plates
* white glue
* aluminum foil
* paper bowl
* clear tape
* pencil
* cotton swabs
* scissors
* poster paint
* paintbrush
* buttons or sequins
* construction paper (optional)
* pipe cleaners (optional)
* craft sticks (optional)

What you will do:

A)

1. Glue two paper plates together and cover them with aluminum foil (See A). Cover a paper bowl with foil. Glue or tape the paper bowl to the top of the paper plates. Let dry.

2. Make landing gear for your spacecraft. Ask an adult to help you

poke four holes in the bottom plate with a pencil. Cut two cotton swabs in half. Paint them black, and let dry. Put glue on the top half of the cotton swabs, and push them into the holes in the plate (See B). Let dry.

B)

3. Glue colorful buttons or sequins around the rim of your spacecraft (See C), and let dry. If you wish, add details using construction paper, pipe cleaners, or craft sticks.

C)

4. What other types of spacecraft can you make?

D)

PATTERNS

Arrowhead Bracelet

At 100%

Use tracing paper to copy the patterns on these pages. Ask an adult to help you cut and trace the shapes.

"I Have a Dream" Rainbow Magnet

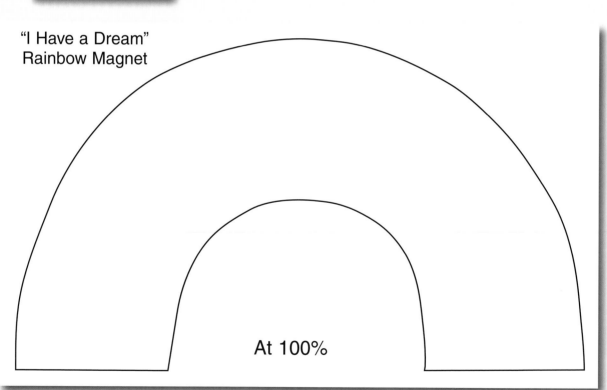

At 100%

Monarch Butterfly "Stained Glass" Chip Clip

At 100%

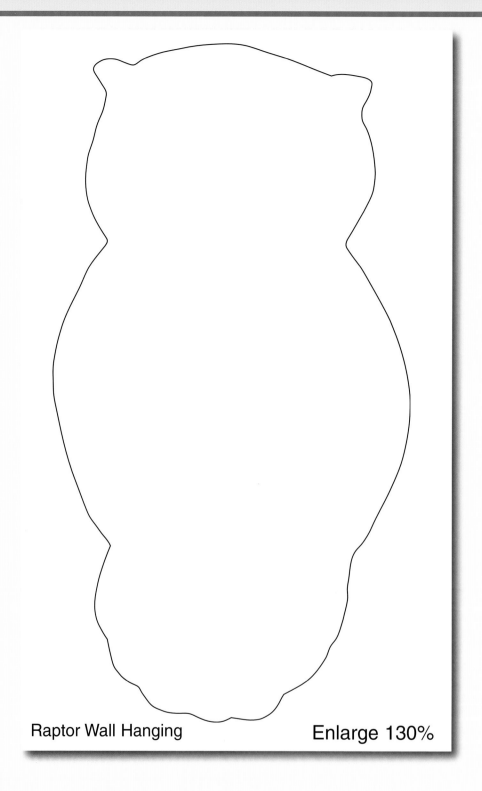

Raptor Wall Hanging

Enlarge 130%

LEARN MORE

Books

Barrett, Tracy. *Virginia.* New York: Benchmark Books, 2004.

Bograd, Larry. *Uniquely Georgia.* Chicago: Heinemann Library, 2004.

Chui, Patricia. *Florida, the Sunshine State.* Milwaukee, WI: World Almanac Library, 2002.

Heinrichs, Ann. *North Carolina.* Minneapolis, Minn.: Compass Point Books, 2003.

Hess, Debra. *South Carolina.* New York: Benchmark Books/Marshall Cavendish, 2004.

Hodgkins, Fran. *West Virginia.* Mankato, Minn.: Capstone Press, 2004.

Internet Addresses

50states.com
    <http://www.50states.com/>

U.S. States
    <http://www.enchantedlearning.com/usa/states/>

INDEX

A

Arrowhead Bracelet, 24

B

Basket Weaving, 28
Big Cypress National
    Preserve, 40
Blackbeard the Pirate, 30

C

Carolina Raptor Center,
    22
Chattahoochee National
    Forest, 5
Cline, Professor Mark, 16
Coal House, 10

E

Everglades National
    Park, 5

F

Fakahatchee Strand
    State Preserve, 40
Florida, 38
Florida Keys, 5
Florida Panther Diorama,
    40
Florida State Flag, 38
Florida State Symbols,
    39
Funny Fantasy Found
    Object Spacecraft, 42

G

Georgia, 32
Georgia State Flag, 32

Georgia State Symbols,
    33
Great Smoky Mountains
    National Park, 4
Gullah community, 28

H

Haunted Monster
    Museum, 16

I

"I Have a Dream"
    Rainbow Magnet, 34
Indian Museum of the
    Carolinas, 24

J

Jolly Roger Pirate Flag,
    30

K

Kennedy Manned Space
    Flight Center, 42
King Jr., Dr. Martin
    Luther, 34

M

McRae, Georgia, 36
Monarch Butterfly
    "Stained Glass" Chip
    Clip, 12
My Pirate Flag, 30

N

North Carolina, 20
North Carolina State
    Flag, 20

North Carolina State
    Symbols, 21

P

Poe, Edgar Allan, 18
Poe Museum, 18
Poe's Raven, 18

R

Raptor Wall Hanging, 22

S

Scary Monster, 16
Sea Islands, 28
Shenandoah National
    Park, 5
South Carolina, 26
South Carolina State
    Flag, 26
South Carolina State
    Symbols, 27
Southeastern States
    Geography, 4
Statue of Liberty, 36

V

Virginia, 14
Virginia State Flag, 14
Virginia State Symbols,
    15

W

West Virginia, 8
West Virginia State Flag,
    8
West Virginia State
    Symbols, 9